I am the Lorax. I speak for the trees.

—from *The Lorax*

The editors would like to thank
SUSAN ROBERTS, PhD,
Director, Ocean Studies Board
National Academies of Sciences,
Engineering and Medicine,
for her assistance in the preparation of this book.

All rights reserved. Published in the United States by Random House Children's Books,
a division of Penguin Random House LLC, New York. Featuring characters from
The Lorax, ® & copyright © 1971, and copyright renewed 1999 by Dr. Seuss Enterprises, L.P.

Random House and the colophon are registered trademarks of Penguin Random House LLC.

All photographs used under license from Shutterstock.com, with the following exceptions:
New Zealand Whale & Dolphin Trust, p. 20 (top two photographs); Dr. Steve I. Lonhart, NOAA
Monterey Bay National Marine Sanctuary, pp. 32–33.

Visit us on the Web!
Seussville.com
rhcbooks.com

Educators and librarians, for a variety of teaching tools, visit us at RHTeachersLibrarians.com

Library of Congress Cataloging-in-Publication Data is available upon request.
ISBN 978-0-593-56521-6 (trade) — ISBN 978-0-593-56522-3 (lib. bdg.)

MANUFACTURED IN CHINA

10 9 8 7 6 5 4 3 2 1

First Edition

Random House Children's Books supports the First Amendment and celebrates the right to read.

The LORAX Dr. Seuss

What Humming-Fish Wish

How YOU Can Help Protect Sea Creatures

by Michelle Meadows

illustrated by Aristides Ruiz

Random House 🏠 New York

I am the Lorax.
Let's go to the sea!
I invite you to come
on a journey with me.

Deep down in the water
and up on the shore,
sea creatures need help
more than ever before.

Some animals have
a special distinction.
ENDANGERED means they
are at risk of extinction.

When threats to survival
get worse or persist,
it means a whole species
may cease to exist.

Here is a fact that
we must all understand.
What goes on in the ocean
affects us on land.

The ocean provides us
with clean air and heat.
It also provides us
with food that we eat.

When one species disappears,
it hurts other species, too.
Helping all species survive
is what we need to do!

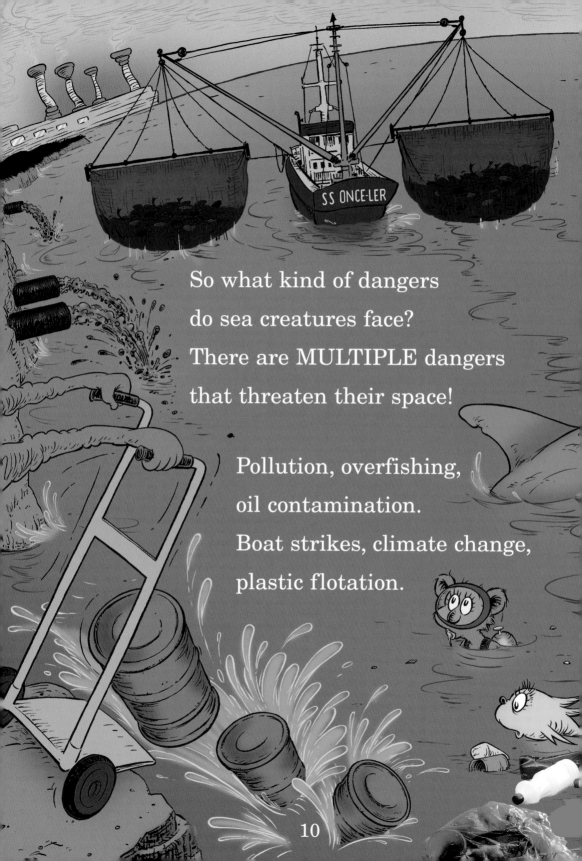

So what kind of dangers
do sea creatures face?
There are MULTIPLE dangers
that threaten their space!

Pollution, overfishing,
oil contamination.
Boat strikes, climate change,
plastic flotation.

This sounds like a LOT,
and it is, this is true.
But if we work together,
there's a LOT we can do!

I'd like you to meet
some good friends of mine.
They're endangered, but we
can help stop their decline.

Hungry hawksbill turtles
out hunting for lunch
think plastic looks like
something tasty to munch.

It clogs up their bellies!
Gets stuck in their throats!
It's a danger to turtles
wherever it floats.

Do you want to help them?
Here's what you can do:
start using less plastic
and recycle, too.

Blue whales are the biggest!
What a marvelous tail!
But injuries happen
when a boat hits a whale.

Boaters should watch
for blue whales on the go.
And they need to slow down
if they see a whale blow.

Did you know?
One way whales talk to one another is
by slapping the water with their tails.

Collisions with boats
harm whales every year.
Whales also get tangled
in ghost fishing gear.

Ghost gear is discarded,
abandoned at sea,
trapping sea creatures
who cannot break free.

17

The great bluefin tuna
is a large bony fish
sought after for sushi—
a popular dish.

Did you know?
Most fish reproduce, or have offspring,
by laying eggs.

But bluefin are fished faster
than they can reproduce.
And overfishing like this
is a kind of abuse.

Avoid eating fish if
its species has declined.
Try to eat fish
that are easy to find!

19

Hector's dolphins surf waves
on New Zealand's coast.
Fishing nets are the threat
that affects them the most.

Bycatch are sea creatures
that get caught by mistake.
The nets catch more species
than they're meant to take.

The mesh in the nets
can hold dolphins down.
They get injured or tangled,
and some of them drown.

Safe fishing practices
let dolphins swim free.
They need our protection.
That's how it should be!

Whale sharks' mouths open wide—
sometimes up to five feet—
to catch food in their gills.
This is how whale sharks eat.

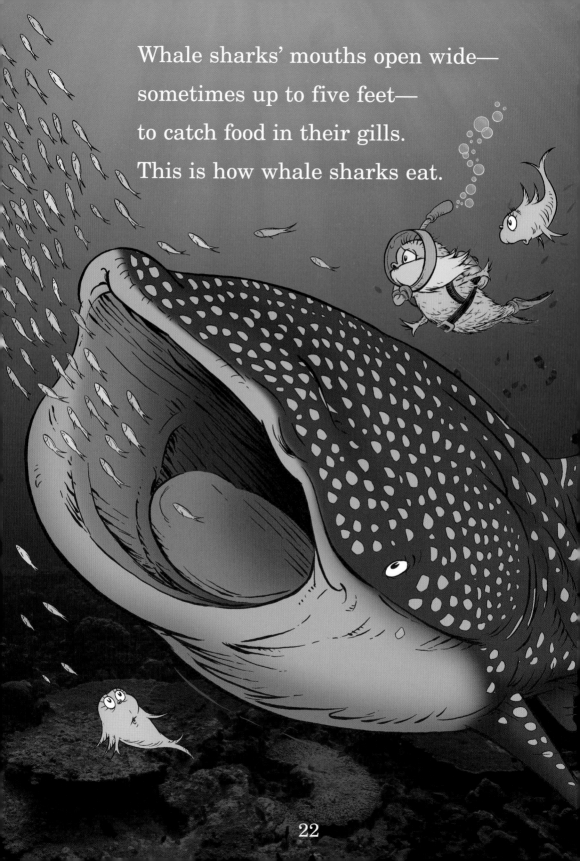

But fishing and bycatch
have made their numbers drop.
The taking of these gentle giants
simply HAS TO STOP!

Did you know?
The pattern on a whale shark's back is
as unique as a human fingerprint!

23

Although it may look
like a plant quite a lot,
coral is an ANIMAL,
believe it or not!

And INSIDE of coral
(you will think this is neat)
is a plant we call algae—
it makes food corals eat!

Did you know?
Coral gets its color from the algae
inside it.

Coral shelters the algae,
so together they thrive
in reefs large and small
you can see when you dive!

The staghorn coral,
with branches far reaching,
suffers because of
sea coral bleaching.

As Earth's climate changes,
water temperatures rise.
And the more it heats up,
the more coral reef dies.

Warm ocean water
creates quite a sight.
Coral spits out the algae
and turns totally white!

26

In this ghostly state,
most coral will die.
Coral needs algae
for its food supply.

The huge humphead wrasse
is a coral reef creature
with a bulge on its forehead—
an eye-catching feature!

This big, beautiful fish
calls the reef home, sweet home.
It is where wrasse find food
and a safe place to roam.

When the climate is too hot
for the reef habitat,
there's no home for the wrasse,
and we must prevent that!

The Siberian sturgeon
is fished for its roe—
the eggs inside females
that would otherwise grow.

Roe is eaten as food—
it's called caviar.
Expensive fish eggs
in a tin or a jar.

CAVIAR

Because of demand,
this fish is now rare.
But there are ways we can
treat sturgeons with care.

One way we can help?
Provide special places
where sturgeons can breed
in protected spaces.

31

The black abalone
is a plant-eating snail
with shimmering shells
that range dark to pale.

Their numbers are low,
I am sorry to say.
And although it's illegal,
they're still hunted today.

Taking abalone
is mollusk misuse!
We must leave them alone
so they can reproduce.

The LONE in ABALONE
sounds like the word BONY.
Say it out loud.
It rhymes with BALONEY!

I speak for sea creatures
from huge whales to small fish.
We must act to protect them.
That's what Humming-Fish wish!

Bring reusable bags
when you go to the store.
That's easy to do—
and here's something more:

Reuse containers.
Don't use plastic straws.
Let's keep plastic trash
out of sea creatures' jaws!

To help conserve water,
you can shorten your shower.
And unplug sometimes
to use up less power.

Want to help keep the ocean
from getting too hot?
Walk and ride your bike more—
small things mean a LOT!

We ALL can be part
of a problem's solution—
from boat strikes to bycatch,
plastic to pollution.

The more you can do
and the more that you know,
endangered sea creatures
will flourish and grow.

Be a green superhero!
It's well within reach.
Here are steps you can take
to **CLEAN UP A BEACH.**

Step 1: With an adult's help,
recruit a team. Work with
friends and family, or reach out
to your school or community.

Step 2: Identify a cleanup site. Not
everyone lives near the ocean, but ponds,
lakes, and rivers need our help, too!

Step 3: Gather supplies. You'll need:

- Trash bags, baskets, or pails for collecting garbage and recyclables
- Gloves

- Sunscreen
- Bug spray
- Drinking water
- Hand sanitizer
- First aid kit

Some tips:
- Wear comfortable shoes that you don't mind getting wet.
- Ask an adult to pick up any fishing tackle you find. It's likely to have a sharp hook!
- Plan your cleanup for when the beach won't be crowded or too hot.
- Take pictures! Spread the word about the importance of keeping the beach clean.

For More Information

Just like the Lorax, YOU can be a caring marine conservationist. Get involved in efforts to help and save endangered sea creatures. Learn more by checking out these websites:

The **California Academy of Sciences** provides sustainable fishing games and activities, allowing kids to explore how fishing affects marine life.

calacademy.org/educators/lesson-plans/sustainable-fishing

Find Your Blue at the Smithsonian Ocean Portal features resources for parents and caregivers on how to help kids protect the ocean, including videos, action steps, and service projects related to the ocean.

ocean.si.edu/conservation/get-involved/helping-kids-help-ocean

Greenpeace highlights environmental programs and promotes a green and peaceful future. They offer lesson plans, field trip ideas, games, and other materials for kids of all ages.

greenpeace.org/international/campaign/toolkit-plastic-free-future /tools-for-teachers/

The **Marine Bio Conservation Society** (MarineBio) promotes education about ocean life and marine conservation. The MarineBio kids' site offers fun facts, games, and puzzles.

marinebio.org/kids

The **Marine Stewardship Council** advances sustainable fishing and offers ocean sustainability videos, games, and other learning activities for kids.

msc.org/en-us/teachers-and-parents-ocean-sustainability

The **National Oceanic and Atmospheric Administration** (NOAA) offers a variety of great resources for parents, educators, and kids. Find fun activities, including coloring sheets, puzzles, games, science projects, and videos.

oceanservice.noaa.gov/kids/

> **Fishwatch.gov**—a service of NOAA—offers a Fish Finder search tool to help you make smart seafood choices at the grocery store, as well as information about what makes seafood sustainable.
>
> fishwatch.gov
>
> **Sea Grant** is a NOAA program that hosts a variety of ocean science education resources, including activities and lesson plans, for home and classroom use.
>
> seagrant.noaa.gov/educationathome

Glossary

Bycatch: Marine animals caught unintentionally by fishing gear.

Cease: To stop or come to an end.

Climate change: Significant and long-lasting change in weather and seasonal patterns, including related changes in ocean temperature.

Coral reef: Large underwater structures composed of the skeletons of marine invertebrates called coral.

Decline: When a population becomes smaller in number of individuals.

Distinction: A special quality that sets something apart.

Endangered: Seriously at risk of extinction.

Extinction: When a species or group of animals is no longer in existence.

Ghost fishing gear: Discarded, lost, or abandoned fishing gear that continues to trap marine life in the ocean.

Habitat: The natural home for a plant, animal, or insect.

Overfishing: Harvesting more fish than can be taken sustainably, leading to depletion of the stock.

Persist: To continue.

Pollution: The presence in the environment of a harmful or poisonous substance.

Reproduce: To duplicate or to have offspring, or babies.

Species: Classification of living things into groups that are most alike. For example, bluefin tuna is one species of fish and humphead wrasse is another species of fish.

Index

algae, 24–27

beach cleanup, 38–39
black abalone, 32–33
blue whales, 14–15
bluefin tuna, 18–19
boat strikes, 10, 14–16, 37
bycatch, 20–21, 23, 37

caviar, 30
climate change, 10, 26, 28, 36
coral reefs, 24–28

dolphins, 20–21

endangered species, 7, 11, 37
extinction, 7

fish, 18–19, 28–31, 34
fishing, 10, 16–21, 23, 30–31,
    37, 39

ghost fishing gear, 16–17, 39

hawksbill turtles, 12–13
Hector's dolphins, 20–21
humphead wrasse, 28

ocean, importance of, 8
oil spills, 10
overfishing, 10, 18–19, 30–31

plastic, 10, 12–13, 35, 37
pollution, 10, 12–13, 37

recycling, 13, 39

sharks, 22–23
Siberian sturgeons, 30–31
snails, 32–33
staghorn coral, 26
sushi, 18

turtles, 12–13

whale sharks, 22–23
whales, 14–17, 34

The LORAX
Dr. Seuss

Encourage a love of nature
and respect for the environment in children of ALL ages
with these other books featuring Dr. Seuss's Lorax!